THE
RING FINDER

THE
RING FINDER

HOW TO MAKE A PROFIT WITH
YOUR METAL DETECTOR

STEVE ZAZULYK

Editor: Lacy Lieffers, One Leaf Editing

Cover and interior design: Meghan Behse

Cover photograph: Natalie Roessler Photography

ISBN 978-1-9991398-0-3 (paperback)
ISBN 978-1-9991398-1-0 (ebook)

Table of Contents

I was able to relive my days of motocross racing by driving one of these dirt bikes through the woods and swamps to the original "drop zone" to find this platinum wedding ring.

In honor of my father

While recovering rings for your clients, don't be surprised to find unexpected treasures like these beautiful vintage rings.

This huge gold ring was lost and found *twice* for the owner; only a year apart and at the same beach.

This 1967 10k gold class ring, with an Alaskan black diamond, was found while detecting on a beach.

Introduction:
The Ring Finder

By the beginning of 2019, I had made over $100,000—by finding lost rings. Not bad for a part-time hobby, considering most people don't even know what a "ring finder" is.

Quite simply, a ring finder is an individual who is hired to use a metal detector to find a lost ring and is often rewarded for their efforts. It's a growing hobby, and if you know what to do, can be a lucrative service. To be quite honest, I actually stumbled into ring finding after years of being an amateur metal detectorist. I had a neighbor who, three years prior, had lost a ring that was extremely sentimental to him. He asked if my metal detector could find silver. Fortunately, I had grown confident in my detector and knew how to differentiate between the varying tones and signals of metal, aluminum, gold, and silver, so I thought I'd give it a try...and thankfully, I did! To everyone's amazement, including my own, the second target I ran my detector over rang true for silver; however, it indicated that the "target" was at a depth of three inches. Slightly skeptical that the ring could have traveled that far underground in such a short period of time, I proceeded to dig it out. Little did I know how much my life was going to change the moment I flipped over that plug of soil—revealing a very dirty, but still beautiful, silver ring.

Soon after, others heard about the recovery and began approaching me to help find rings (or other types of jewellery) they had lost days or even years ago. Each with a story of their own: a family heirloom buried on a property; a $40,000 diamond engagement ring lost at the beach; a $30,000 earring recovered from a golf course; a platinum wedding ring pitched into a pond after a lovers' quarrel (wow, the money I've made from those). I have watched some of the most unbelievable stories unfold; witnessing people go from their lowest moment of loss and despair, to pure elation—all because I had found their lost ring. With ring finding, I have been lucky to be part of so many of these moments and have included pictures of some of my most memorable finds throughout this book.

People started reaching out to me in every city, town, and country I visited, and they were willing to offer me anything from apple pie to money as a thanks. The more rings I found, the more I began seeing it as a potentially lucrative service and increased my focus on it. Seeing the wonderful opportunity, I re-certified myself as a diver and was able to locate lost rings on land as well as in the water. By 2019, I had recovered hundreds of rings (as well as keys, cell phones, drones, and even buried money) in over twenty countries. My gratuities were now averaging between $300 to $600 a find on land, and between $800 to $1,200 per water hunt or scuba dive recovery (with the highest gratuity offered at $5,000, for a single ring). I was accepting an average of ten requests a week and up to five calls a day in the busy winter and beach months. What began as favor for a friend, had grown into a viable gratuity-based service, and I was making quite a name for myself in the process!

I started receiving offers from around the globe to detect with some of the best treasure hunters on the planet. In 2014, I was invited onto the first season of History Channels' *The Curse of Oak Island*. It was on this show, that I used my skills to find the first verified piece of treasure in the history of the island: a 300-year-old pirate coin. That coin helped catapult the series to the number one History Channel docuseries of all time and elevated my status as a professional treasure hunter. In time, I was being asked to speak on the topic of detecting and to share my "treasured" skills to groups of soon-to-be ring finders in Canada, the United States, and Europe. Most recently, I have become a regular columnist for a major treasure hunting magazine, *American Digger*, with my column "Below the Surface."

People, podcasters, and fellow hobbyists who watched my "live" social media recoveries, or saw me on T.V., wanted to learn what I did and how I did it. Turning the hobby of metal detecting into a profitable service was something many were interested in.

It has been a truly amazing journey; though when I started, I had no idea about detectors, I didn't know what equipment was needed, which techniques were best to use, or as things progressed how to advertise my service. It's been an exciting learning process the entire way; one that anyone can follow, if they are serious. In fact, you might even have an advantage over me. When I first started, there weren't a lot of people in the hobby, and there were no books to buy, podcasts you could listen to, or social media pages to follow. At the time, there was only you, your detector, and the information you could glean from someone else willing enough to share it.

Requests for a ring finding service are growing by the day, and detectorists are unable to keep up with the public demand. I realized that I had acquired a skill that could be of value to new people interested in the hobby and have made it my undertaking to give back and mentor the next generation of ring finders. It was through that desired passion that I decided to write this book. As the literal guide to ring finding, it is my intended goal that it will save you years of having to learn from your own mistakes, by listening to the lessons learned from mine—although, you no doubt will learn from your own as well. Through the years, I have invested far more (than I ever made) on purchasing new equipment and traveling the world to further develop my skills and to promote the hobby. In all honesty, my sincerest hope is that you become an even better ring finder than I am!

I wanted to write a book that didn't beat around the bush and gave the real "nuts and bolts" about the hobby, from beginning to end. In this book, you will learn what equipment to use (on land or in the water), which techniques work best, and how to navigate through each situation, from advertising your service and the initial contact, to locating the ring and receiving your gratuity. Knowing the right metal detector programmable settings and grid patterns can make the difference between a successful ring find, and a fruitless one. By the end of this book, you will have the knowledge required to help start your own successful ring finding service.

Hired to find this platinum ring in a quarry's swimming hole. While on the find, I also found this Last Supper solid gold pendant — a great bonus for the day's work.

These three beautiful gold rings were unexpectedly found while on another successful platinum ring find for a client.

A 1942 silver Walking Liberty half dollar. One of the many relics you might also find while ring finding.

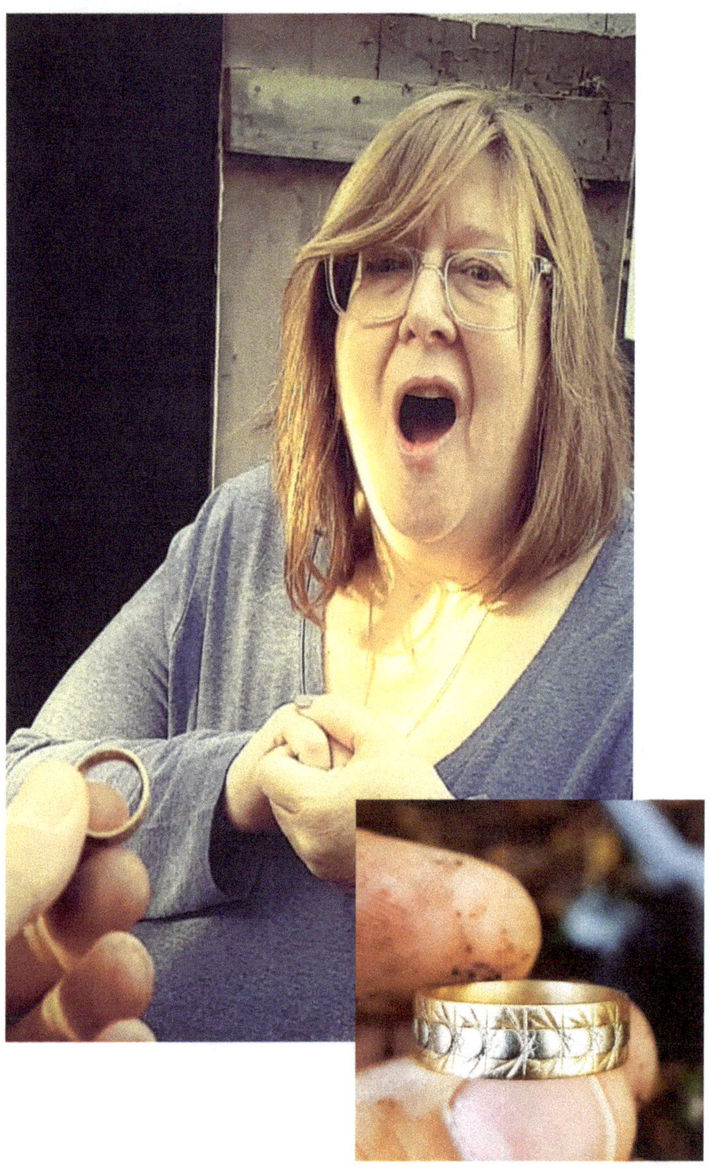

This lady was shocked after I found her mother's wedding band, that was lost twenty years earlier. I found the ring on the final day before their property was sold.

1
Let's Get Started: The Basics About Detectors

To be a successful ring finder, you need the right equipment. There are a few things you should include in your "tool kit," but there's no better place to start than with the star of the show: the metal detector. If you already own one and know how to use it, then congratulations—you're already over the first hurdle and can skip ahead to Chapter 2 that lists what other equipment this hobby requires. For those of you that need to buy a metal detector, this chapter is a great starting point.

COMPONENTS OF A METAL DETECTOR

As shown in the diagram, there are six main components of a metal detector: control box, shaft, search coil, display, arm cuff, and headphones. Understanding the significance of each is key to properly using your metal detector. Use the diagrams and descriptions on the following pages to familiarize yourself with the different components of a metal detector and how they work together to find a target.

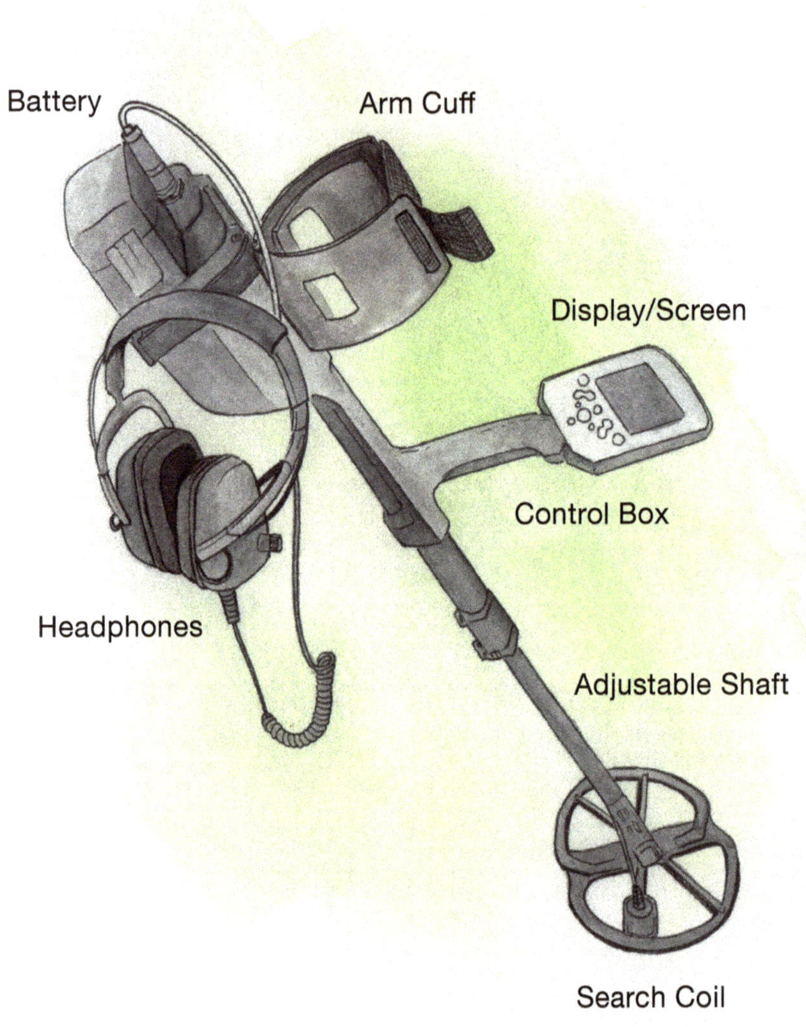

Components – Land-based Metal Detector

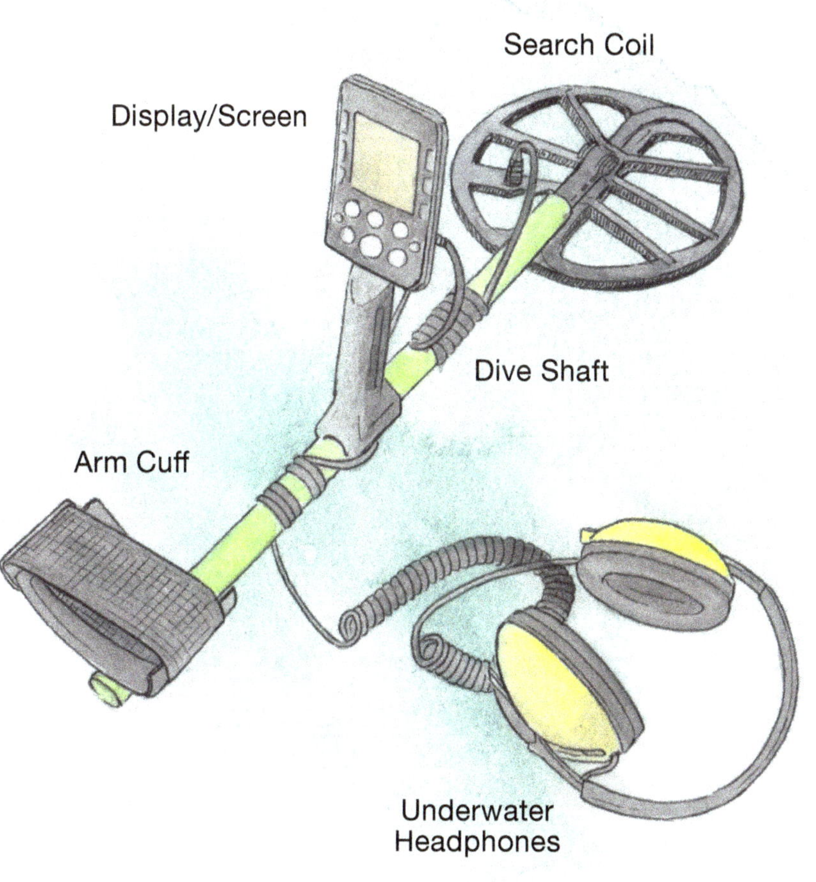

Components – Water-based Metal Detector

Control Box

Think of this unit as the brains or hard drive of your detector. It houses the battery, microprocessor, and controls. The detector is unable to function without it.

Shaft

Basically, it's the long pole on your detector. Consider it the spine that everything connects to. The shaft is made from materials such as aluminum, fibreglass composite, or carbon fibre that make the detector light and easy to handle, yet rigid and durable. The aluminum and fibreglass composite are the less expensive options, but they are heavier than carbon fibre. For an extremely lightweight and durable shaft, one made of carbon fibre is recommended.

The shaft comes in two parts: the upper and lower sections. These two sections make the shaft adjustable, allowing the user to match it to their height as well as the intended use of the machine. Shorter shafts are best for diving and detecting in water; whereas, a longer shaft is best for detecting on land.

Search Coil

Also known as the coil head, this is the most essential part of your detector. This flat, (typically) circular disk uses a magnetic field to detect metallic targets. Located at the end of your shaft, it connects to the control box via an electric cable. To install this cable properly, wrap it over top of the shaft, starting from the bottom and moving towards the control box. Use cable ties to keep it securely in place. Proper installation will prevent the rotation of the coil head from pinching and eventually damaging the cable, while still allowing full pivoting range of your coil head.

PROTIP

To decrease interference and have your machine run at optimal performance, create distance between the majority of the cable around the shaft and the coil head itself by winding the cable as high up the shaft as possible, while still allowing the search coil to pivot freely.

Display/Screen

Located by the control box, the purpose of the screen is to give visual information about your targets. The numbers shown will help you correctly identify your target. For example, a gold target will be displayed as the number "15" on your screen. Most land detectors come equipped with screens, but it's common for water machines to instead use only tone detector technology, where you must listen and discern between the different sounds and signals of your targets. Chapter 4 examines the tones associated with different types of ferrous and non-ferrous metal targets.

Arm Cuff

Your forearm rests inside the arm cuff component of the metal detector. Using a strap to keep it secured around your arm, it helps to reduce neck and arm strain and keeps the detector steady as you sweep it back and forth.

Headphones

Optional, but recommended to hear the information the detector is receiving. Headphones will allow you to hear small targets deep in the ground, that audio from the main speaker may miss. They also keep you and the machine quiet if you ever have to detect around people. Nothing is more irritating than having a ring finder near you, with no headphones on and a constant beeping noise coming from their machine. Headphones do come in a waterproof option, for submersible recoveries.

SELECTING A DETECTOR

When it comes to actually selecting a metal detector, a vast array of machines exist on the market today. Just like any other tool or piece of equipment, prices vary depending on the use, capability, and level of functionality you want from the unit. You want to base your decision upon where your primary source of ring finding will be. Metal detecting can be done either on land or in the water, and there are machines made specifically for each, with a select few being able to perform in both surroundings. The machines that operate in both environments use a different technology than a strictly land-based machine, and as a result, their prices are often higher. Chapter 10 discusses what to look for in a detector and other equipment, when ring finding in the water.

Mid-range land detectors, worth between $300-$500 in today's market, are a great investment for those new to the hobby. Nothing will turn you off metal detecting faster than a cheap detector, so invest in one that fits your skill level and your budget, and avoid the low-end $100 machines. Mid-range detectors have enough functionality for you to "learn the ropes" and gain comfort with your new machine, in a cost-effective way. As your skills progress, you might want to graduate to a water-based detector or a higher-end land detector that has more depth capability. The most important thing is that you are comfortable with your machine and understand that it takes time to develop your skill, so select a machine that fits your budget and is easy to use.

PURCHASING: ONLINE, OR LOCAL STORE?

Each have their own merits, and choosing to purchase your metal detector online or from your local store comes down to your personal preference and comfort level. If you have time for it, buying online can be an excellent way to save money on a good-quality machine. There are many dealers that will also sell their equipment online. Due to the volume of sales and online promotions, you can often get a machine cheaper than what you could buy it for, direct from the store.

To ensure you buy a machine online that you know you will be happy with, it's a good idea to first find a dealer you like that also sells their equipment online so you can test out the different detectors and then watch for online deals. I've seen instances where the machines and equipment are up to 20% less. If your budget is somewhat limited, you can go online and look for a used metal detector—but buyer beware. There are many horror stories about people purchasing used metal detectors and not receiving what was advertised. I was one of those unfortunate individuals, and in one instance I received a metal detector that did not work. The best way to avoid this is to actually meet with the individual (prior to purchasing the detector) so they can walk you through it and so you can see the machine is working. This is also advisable as the owner will have experience with the machine and will be able to tell you about any issues or instructions you may not be aware of.

The advantage of purchasing direct from a dealer is the face-to-face customer relationship you establish, when you find a dealer you trust. If you have any issues or questions with your machine, or need help setting it up, they will be your best resource. They are well-versed in the capabilities of each detector, and are very helpful and informative. If you can afford a new machine, then purchasing direct from a dealer is your best way to gain that extra level of support as you grow in this hobby.

My first five-gold-ring day, which included the beautiful "Mizpah" ring at center that had a date of 1897 inscribed on the inside.

These two rings are authentic Italian gold and were recovered off of a beach near Cinque Terre, Italy.

This beautiful emerald ring was found using "the Dorothy" spiral search pattern.

This young man had faith that I would find his grandfather's ring—even though his mother said she was "sure it had gone over Niagara Falls by now!" Thanks to the "mowing the lawn" search pattern, this beautiful 18k gold family heirloom was put back on his hand, only minutes after arriving.

2

The Ring Finder's Toolkit

Aside from a metal detector, there are many other tools of the trade that will help you become a professional ring finder. The types of tools and equipment you select, much like with a detector, depends largely upon where you will be performing your ring finding services. This chapter focuses on the overall (land) equipment needed for ring finders; whereas, Chapter 10 gives an in-depth look of what it takes—and what you need—to dive detect or search in the water. Being a ring finder does not require a lot of equipment, but these are the things you need to keep in mind and on-hand, when hunting on land.

Shovel

A ring won't always be laying on or close to the top of the ground, and every once in a while, you may have to dig for them. Having a small garden or hand shovel with you will help you retrieve the target while reducing the amount of surface area you have to dig up. Keep in mind that for those larger items, or in tougher spots, you will need a stronger shovel or spade for cutting through the ground. Just be respectful when digging up property. Replace what you dug up, and if possible, add some water to the spot to prevent the grass from dying.

Rake

A garden rake can be an immense help at a ring find—and not just for clearing the area from loose debris. On fall finds, you can use it to rake up a pile of grass or leaves in the drop zone (where the ring was presumed to have been dropped) and then detect the pile. Sometimes, the ring will pop right out of the ground once the rake goes over top of it. In winter, you can use this same method to rake the snow into a pile before detecting it, or you can use it to rake off the new layer of fallen snow to search the ground underneath.

Traffic Cones

Cones, or some sort of visible driveway marker, are a great way to plot out your search area. You can find small versions of these at most dollar stores, making it easy to stock up at a reasonable price.

Pinpointer Probe

A pinpointer probe is a small, handheld version of a metal detector. Once you detect a target (with your metal detector) use the pinpointer to zero in on its exact location. The tip of these contains an electro-magnetic probe that will alert you, by vibration or audio signal, when you are in close proximity to your target. This will help decrease digging time by reducing the size of hole you need to dig. They come in a variety of models, with a basic version starting at $50, up to a waterproof unit with adjustable sensitivity, priced around $150.

Camera

Though not required, a camera (or phone) is always a good thing to have on hand on a hunt. As discussed in Chapters 5 and 9, the best way to promote your service is by taking quality photos and videos of your finds.

Footwear

When it comes to ring finding, one of the most important things you want to protect is your feet. You will be searching on many different types of terrain, and there can be many hidden dangers such as rusty nails, glass, and snakes (depending on where you search). Ideally, a hard-toe boot with a steel shank would be perfect, but unfortunately, as that metal detector you have in your hand will go off every time you swing it by your feet, it's recommended to instead find a sturdy, shin-height boot with a high-strength plastic toe. When the weather is severe, you should invest in an insulated winter boot. Nothing worse than showing up to a ring find and you can't even last five minutes because your feet feel like two blocks of ice.

Pants

Pants, pants, pants. No matter how warm it is outside, that word should sound through your head whenever you're getting ready to go out on a land recovery. Purchase some outdoor pants that are designed for hunters or hikers. These types of pants not only protect your legs against cuts, scrapes, and infectious plants, but they are designed to stretch in all the right areas and are semipermeable, allowing proper air flow so you won't sweat and become uncomfortable.

Knee Pads

For those both young and old, these are a must for protecting your knees from strains and injuries. You will be kneeling thousands of times throughout your career, and further to the point of hidden dangers, you need to be extremely cautious when you're kneeling on the ground. Anything could cut or bruise your knee, and once it does, the ring find could be over. I've actually been only minutes away from a ring finding destination and turned my vehicle around when I realized I had forgotten my knee pads. A gel-filled ballistic polyester knee pad, that you can buy at most big box home improvement retailers, is your best friend when it comes to protecting your knees for years to come.

Shirts and Upper Body Wear

Considering that you could be called out in all seasons, your upper-body clothing is crucial. Layers are the most important thing for the unpredictable weather in the winter months. Semipermeable clothing is best for regulating your body temperature while allowing the material to breathe. There are some amazing light-weight raincoats and hiking jackets available to keep you warm and dry and allow you the freedom to move. Once the warmer weather hits, it's tempting to wear shorter-sleeves, but it's important to keep your upper body protected. A long-sleeved t-shirt, with a good wicking material, will protect you from sunburns, cuts, and bug bites and will not cause you to over-heat. You can find some very comfortable and stylish shirts from any running or hiking store that are made to regulate body heat and protect you from the elements.

Hats

Hats are a matter of preference but are a great way to protect the top of your head from the sun, as well as keep the hair off your face. A great option for ring finders are the hats that have a small light embedded in the peak. These are especially beneficial when you are looking for a ring later on in the day and start to lose light. Of course, you can also invest in a headlamp to wear, to give additional light for those later hunts.

Gloves

It cannot be said enough that protecting your body on a ring find is critical to your safety, and it doesn't stop at your hands. A form-fitting pair of high-dexterity gloves are essential for protecting your hands from those hidden dangers.

This near-flawless diamond engagement ring was thought to have been lost in the owner's yard. Only after hearing the story in detail, did I realize that she may have lost it across town in her friend's driveway. Tears of joy and utter shock appeared when I pulled this ring from the snowbank.

3

Tips, Tricks, and Techniques

Before you begin ring finding, you need to make sure your metal detector is set up for optimal performance. It cannot be expressed strong enough that good care and maintenance of your detector is the best way to ensure the longevity of your machine. Prior to assembling your detector, make sure you read the manual and familiarize yourself with it. The manuals are included for a reason, and there are so many things that you can learn about your detector regarding tone and signal identification, detection depth, and sensitivity—before you switch it on.

For those that want to "tread the water before diving in," you'll be happy to know that your detector will come pre-programmed with factory settings that are designed to locate desirable targets and "null" the bad ones. To start, don't worry too much about the settings on your detector—focus on getting comfortable with the machine. Most ring finding can be achieved by using the "coin finding" or "ring finding" settings on your detector.

Once you become more proficient with the abilities of your machine and want to dig deeper into its settings, you can either refer back to the manual or ask your dealer to help you set it up and explain the different settings. Other great resources for learning about any metal detector are YouTube or online metal detecting forums. Both are filled with videos and resources, made by people that have become experts on their own machine, to help you learn more about your particular machine.

DEVELOPING A GOOD SWING

A good swing is just as important in ring finding as it is on the golf course. If you do not swing your detector back and forth properly, the machine will not function effectively, and you will likely miss your target. No matter which search technique you use, **just remember to hold it parallel, move it slow, and keep it tight.** When you swing the search coil over the ground, it must be as parallel to the surface as possible to properly pick up on targets that are directly below you.

To best determine the speed of your swing, simply follow the three second rule and count steamboats or Mississippi's to keep your swing at an honest three seconds for each path, from left to right, or vice versa. Your detector needs time to process information from the ground, and if you swing too fast, you do not allow it the time it needs and might literally miss that $20,000 diamond engagement ring you're looking for…go slow!

When executing the proper swing pattern, your detector should not swing too far out and away from your body. People tend to do this out of excitement for the find, but it is an easy way to cause fatigue and injury in your neck, shoulders, and arms, and it puts you at risk for missing your target by not following your search pattern.

Daisy Cutter

PROTIP

Knowing if the location of your target is either below or above ground will determine the height at which you hold your search coil.

When metal detecting, you typically want to keep your detector low to the ground for those targets buried deep. For rings that have been lost for a few years, this is the suggested height to hold your search coil. However, the majority of requests will come from people who have recently lost their ring, and in all likelihood, the ring you're looking for will be sitting on top of the ground, hidden by grass, sand, or snow. In this instance, it's best to use the "**daisy cutter**" method and swing your search coil six to eight inches above ground—the approximate height of a daisy. Swinging your coil at its maximum height will ensure your detector picks up targets only on the surface. Moreover, it will eliminate interference and signals from soil and sand with a high mineral content, as well as trash and other metallic targets buried beneath, that would otherwise throw you off and slow you down.

SEARCH PATTERNS

Now that you have a good feel and understanding of your metal detector, it's time to learn about the different ring finding techniques. Search patterns, also known as "gridding," are critical for ring finding. Law enforcement use search patterns at crime scenes to help find evidence and other objects or weapons left behind. They know that to have a successful investigation, they must use the proper search pattern.

The same holds true for ring finding, and employing the right search pattern will help you conduct a very systematic and organized search. Each detectorist has their favorite technique, but the three most commonly used are: mowing the lawn, the Dorothy, and the hound dog.

Mowing the Lawn

The simplest and most commonly-used search pattern is called "**mowing the lawn**." This pattern has proven to be one of my most successful and is my go-to upon arrival, whenever possible. When establishing the search area, envision it from above, from a drone's perspective. This way, the possible differences in ground elevation no longer apply. Once done, create a square search pattern in your mind, with the area the ring was lost in (the drop zone) at its center.

Starting at any side that's comfortable, swing in straight lines as you move towards the other end; each time, making a new pass across the drop zone. If you do not have a place of reference at each end of the pass, you can use plastic cones as markers.

When done correctly, this pattern is exactly like mowing the lawn. If after making a full pass in your search area you are unsuccessful, just repeat the process but going in a diagonal direction (just like how your fancy neighbor across the street cuts their grass).

The Dorothy: Spiral Search Pattern

This pattern type is best for when time is of the essence or you're running low on daylight. "**The Dorothy**" is essentially, a circular sweep of the area (think: starting off on the yellow brick road).

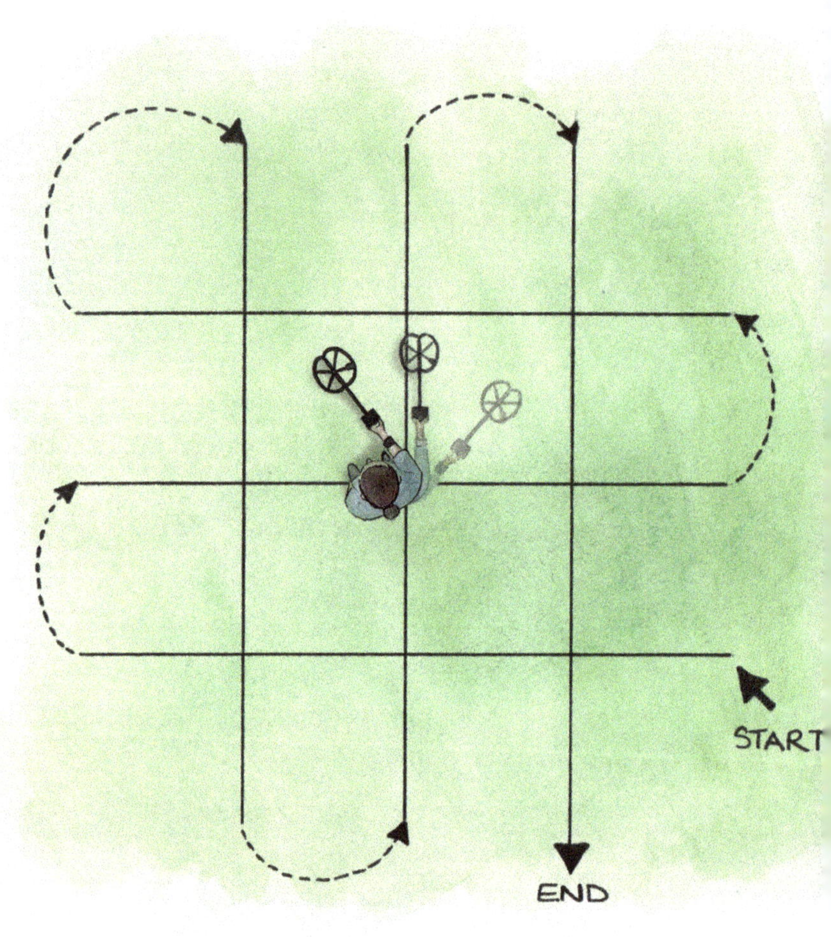

Mowing the Lawn

The Dorothy

Determine the main point you want to start your search from—basically, where your client believes they have lost their ring. Place a marker on this spot and draw an imaginary circle, fifteen feet in diameter (or the size of an above-ground pool), around that spot. This will become your primary search area and is usually referred to as the "golden circle." Then like Dorothy, begin at the center and "follow the yellow brick road," working your way around and away from the marker, in a circular pattern.

The Hound Dog

This search pattern is based on the terrain—and your gut feeling. Reading the surrounding terrain of where a ring was lost is critical in determining how and where to conduct your search. For example, I was once searching for a ring on a snowy trail that had slopes on either side. The woman had lost her ring when she took off her glove and was concerned the ring had fallen off the trail. After a quick assessment of the area, my instinct knew that with such soft snow and the sides not being steep enough for it to roll down, the ring had not traveled far. Trusting my intuition, I proceeded to "**hound dog**" right around the drop area, and sure enough, I found her ring within ten minutes.

Platinum wedding ring recovered by using the "hound dog" search pattern on a steep hiking trail. The woman thought the ring had fallen off the trail, but my instinct knew it could not have traveled far.

My dive partner and I were ecstatic to find forty-seven gold, platinum, and diamond rings after only one week of detecting in Caribbean waters.

This Judo Sensei was convinced that he had lost his wedding ring while laying down sod on his property. However, I was shocked to find his ring in the yard waste container, only moments away from being picked up by the garbage truck.

4

The Sound of Gold

A good ring finder is able to identify the different tones and signals from their detector. The sounds that come from your machine will indicate what the search coil is over, but it's up to you to understand what the target is before digging. If you know the difference between the sound of a gold ring versus that of a beer cap you will significantly reduce the time it takes to locate that ring.

TONES, SOUNDS, AND SIGNALS

Most land metal detectors today will give you two types of information about your target: a number on the display screen (if you have one) and an audible tone. The numbers, or target ID, displayed on the screen will give you more detail on your target. These numbers are different for each manufacturer or metal detector model, so you need to read your user manual to understand what metals the numbers, unique to your machine, indicate.

The tone—or signal—your detector makes, is its way of communicating to you that it has found a target. Every time your detector is swung over a metallic object in the ground, if it is within the detector's capability to detect it, you will hear a signal in your headphones. With a trained ear, that sound will give you all kinds of information about what that target actually is.

The tone from a metal detector is similar to that of a musical note of an instrument, and it can be broken down into three sections: a beginning, middle, and end. All three have distinct sounds, and if you can identify between the different combinations of an approach at the beginning, a sustained middle, and a release at the end, it's what will help you identify the target.

THE SOUND OF GOLD

Yes, gold really makes a sound, and it's unmistakable and beautiful. There are other metals that come close to producing a similar sound, but nothing can really resonate in the same way. When you're over gold, it is a solid, unwavering round signal, that is not choppy, but clear. Almost like listening to a perfect musical note. The "round" signal is referring to a perfect blend of those three parts of a musical note. The combination of which is so smooth, that it actually sounds—round. Odd I know, but trust that after time you will understand what this means.

The three different types of rings you will most commonly search for are gold, silver, and platinum. Gold, as mentioned above, gives a perfectly round signal. The tone for silver is very solid and clear, much like the pitch of an alto singer or small bell, but not quite as melodic as the tenor sound of gold. A platinum ring tone will match the smoothness of a gold signal, but will have a slightly richer finish. Junk targets (such as bottle caps, pull tabs, and iron) are typically irregular in shape, and as a result, will have a choppy and broken sound. Identifying the different tones your detector makes will help you identify between the different ferrous and non-ferrous metal targets in the ground.

FERROUS AND NON-FERROUS METAL TARGETS

Your metal detector is designed to detect for all types of metal in the ground. That metal is divided into two categories, called ferrous and non-ferrous metal. You will be looking for **non-ferrous targets**, such as gold, silver, and platinum (also referred to as precious metals) around 90% of the time. Other non-ferrous metals include titanium, bronze, brass, tin, copper, and unfortunately aluminum. The reason I say "unfortunately aluminum" is because you will learn to hate pull tabs, pop tops, and bottle caps. All three are made of aluminum, and their tone is quite similar to gold. You will be shocked at how much exists in the ground.

Ferrous targets have iron in them and are usually not a desirable target; at least, not when you're searching for a lost ring. Items such as nails, spikes, and scrap metal fall under this category. If these metals are laying on the ground, depending on their size, they can cover the ring, making it impossible to detect. This is why it's critical to clean off any unwanted debris when you arrive to a site, and why it's important to have a rake and a good pair of gloves on hand.

TEST GARDEN

Your success with ring finding will come from how well you know your machine and trust your skills. The best way to practice your search techniques and to learn the different target ID and tones associated with the different rings and other metals you will run across, is to create a "test garden" for yourself.

You can make one of these at home in your backyard, in a spot out in the woods, or at the beach. First plot out an area, then bury coins, rings, and other metal items at various depths, and then practice going over it with your metal detector; using different techniques each time. This is an incredibly helpful tool to learn what techniques you like best, the visual readings and numbers on your display, and the tones of each target.

PROTIP

When testing out your techniques, tie a fishing line to each ring (or metal item) you are burying. Tie knots into the line, at pre-measured distances, and secure the other end to a colourful spool. Place the "targets" into your holes, and fill them up—keeping the spool on top. This allows you to know the exact depth of your practice targets, and ensures you don't lose any of them while practicing your techniques.

This 14k gold ring, with initials over a gorgeous red stone, was located while dive detecting with scuba tanks in twenty feet of water.

Find of a lifetime: This gold Masonic ring with 6 diamonds has long past lost its owner—a high-ranking Master Mason in the 1920's.

An art deco 14k men's ring with a beautiful amethyst stone. Dated from the early 1930s.

No detector needed: Playing basketball landed this beautiful gold ring in the long grass beside the court. The ring caught the corner of my eye while I was conducting my initial safety check.

5

Promoting Your Service

Now that you have mastered your ring finding techniques and are a bona fide "Mozart" when it comes to picking out the different tones of targets, you need to focus on promoting your ring finding service. The absolute best way to get customers today is online: through websites, social media, and classifieds. There are multiple different ring finding groups or websites whose communities you can join and advertise through; allowing you to promote your business without having to take on the large upfront costs yourself. Social media is the best and most cost-effective way of promoting your service, showcasing your skills, and sharing your brand to a larger audience. Online classified advertising services are a great way to capture potential clients from your area, with minimal effort on your end.

SOCIAL MEDIA

The key to having a presence on social media is establishing your brand and building a relationship with your followers.

Influencers gain a large audience in a short amount of time with the right posts. The quality of your photos, the emotions your videos emit, and the information your posts share are what create that "moment" for your audience. You need to get clear on who you are (your mission), what values you want to get across (your vision), who you are speaking to (your audience), and finally, how you are going to speak to them (your key messages). Have a strategy in place to ensure that you are saying and sharing the right things to your audience, and at the times they want to hear it. The ability to grab your audience's attention is largely determined by the posts and videos you share. For more on how to do this, Chapter 9 discusses how you can use both to capture that moment.

ADVERTISING ONLINE

Most online advertising services have a lost and found, or classifieds, section. This is the area where you should advertise. It is usually the first place people will go when they have lost something precious, such as a cell phone, keys, jewelry—or a ring. The psychology behind advertising your service is crucial to helping you write your ad and staying ahead of the pack.

Selecting a Title

When you create your ad, the wording of the title is especially important. People are quickly scanning through multiple ads, and there's a good possibility that other ring finders are advertising on the same site, so you need to make sure your ad stands out. This means that your title needs to be short, to the point, and must tell people exactly what you're doing. All within a few words.

My advertised title usually says, "Lost ring? I'm a Ring Finder♥!" You'll note that there aren't many words used, but a lot is being said. A couple of key triggers are being planted here that will get the attention of your would-be customers. In this matter, triggers are words, phrases, or pictures that prompt (or trigger) an emotion or reaction. You need both to get a potential client to call.

In this example, the first half of the title, including the question mark, is what will first grab their attention. Most ads will just say, "lost ring" which could be read as someone stating that they have lost a ring and need help finding it. Whether that's true of the ad or not, it's up to the interpretation of the person scrolling through the ads. Posing it as a question changes the dynamic of the title so that you are now speaking directly to them, causing them to continue reading the rest of your title.

The second part of the title, "I'm a Ring Finder♥!" is a statement that clearly defines the service you offer and your passion for it. Most people might not know what a ring finder is, but they will identify with the first part of your ad (if they've lost a ring) and will know that, whatever a ring finder is, it's something essential to the situation they're in. The heart itself, while not a mandatory, is something I include, whenever I can. Not every online classified has the ability to add icons to the title, but the one I use, allows me to add a little heart. The heart is just another way to draw the eye of the reader to the title, show my passion for being a ring finder, and help emit that visual stimulus to the reader.

For men and women, losing a ring that holds sentimental value to them is an emotional situation, so anything you can do within that title to grab their attention, define your service, and show your commitment, will go a long way towards receiving that call.

Writing Your Ad

Now that you've grabbed the reader's attention and have them emotionally invested in your ad, it's up to the rest of the ad to (succinctly) explain what a ring finder is, state the services you offer, and discuss your gratuities. As with the title, you need to keep the ad short and to the point. They won't be interested in reading a novel.

People from all walks of life lose their rings. As with any service, understanding your audience is vital in determining how to best define your service. This is your chance to create that connection with them by relating and being able to demonstrate empathy to their situation. The things you say can make or break your chances of landing that call. Understand that they have a problem and are looking for a solution. Use terms and phrases that define what your service has to offer, specific to the situation they're in.

It's also wise to state within the ad that you use a metal detector to find rings. Chapter 6 discusses the "Three Ds" of determining if you should take a job or not, but it's a good idea to use your ad to pre-qualify these calls. You'd be surprised how many calls come from people who have lost a ring in their house, on a bus, or in their car—all places a detector cannot work, because of too much surrounding metal.

> **PROTIP**
>
> **It may seem obvious, but use an online alias and separate ring finder email, and refrain from posting your phone number and home address in your ads—this will eliminate those prank phone calls at midnight and will stop the spam emails from coming to your personal inbox. Be smart, and only divulge personal information to customers once you've developed a rapport and feel comfortable doing so.**

Photography

The way to really tell a story in your ad is through pictures. Pictures are visual evidence of your success and are the quickest way to explain your service, share your story and create a connection to your potential client. Select clear, high-quality photos that grab their attention and showcase the ring and your detector. Chapter 9 talks in more detail on how you can use photos and videos to help build your story.

Gratuities

Quite honestly, you are investing a lot into your service, so you should be compensated for your efforts. Thankfully, most of those contacting you will already have this understanding. If you are expecting money in exchange for your services, your ad should be straightforward and state that it is a gratuity-based service. This will eliminate any doubt of you expecting a reward or gratuity for your effort. You can either include your fee for finds, or you can state that gratuities will be discussed prior to arrival, and then use the methods explained in Chapter 6 to negotiate the deal on the call.

BUSINESS CARDS

Business cards are another important component of advertising your service. They are easy and inexpensive to create online and are a great way to look professional while leaving your information with potential customers, connections, and at past jobs. Things to include are:

- Your name and title (I suggest using the title "Ring Finder")

- Business name and logo (if you have it)

- Icons and certifications you hold

- Contact information

- List of your services

- Social media links/icons for your different pages

The only thing you should not include is a list of your prices, as they will be ever-changing. Add some visual appeal by incorporating color or design implements onto your card. A business card is just one more way to create an impression, so make sure it represents who you are.

One of my favorite pastimes is to hunt for vintage rings on old properties and beaches. This stunning 1939 class ring, with a blue stone, is one of the many reasons why.

An early Saturday morning ring find. This gorgeous ring was found three feet below sand level at the bottom of a lake.

This happy couple is reunited with his stunning bezel set
wedding band.

6

Negotiating the Deal

A phone call is the first connection and human interaction you'll likely have with a potential client and is crucial to building a positive relationship with the person on the other end. Think about your brand and how you want to present yourself, and remember that you are providing a professional service and must conduct yourself as such. Before you take the call, find a nice, quiet place to talk so you can get the information you need while not being interrupted by kids or barking dogs.

When you answer the phone, decide how you want to introduce yourself. A great way to establish your service, and yourself, as a professional is to refer to yourself as a ring finder. For example, I answer my calls with a simple, "Hello! It's Steve, the ring finder." Once on the call, or at any time you deal with that client, whatever you do—do not swear. Nothing will discredit you, your ability, and even the hobby, faster.

The initial conversation is a critical part of the transaction, so it is important to use this time to hear their story and ask the right questions. By the end of a short conversation, you should be able to glean enough information to decide if the job is worth taking or not.

It never fails that within the first thirty seconds of the conversation, they are going to ask what your rates are or how much you charge for your services. At this point, you want to refrain from answering this question, as the answer depends largely upon a few things. More specifically, you want to determine the value of their lost ring along with the cost of your efforts, and charge accordingly. Now, you can't just outright ask what their ring is worth. It's a personal question and they haven't established enough trust in you yet. Moreover, they might believe that once you discover the full value of their ring, you will charge an obscene amount of money to find it. This is where good communication skills come in handy.

THE THREE Ds

When assessing the worth of a ring find, **it boils down to the Three Ds: distance, difficulty, and do they know where it is.** Each of these will influence your decision to take the job and the amount you require for a gratuity.

The first questions you should ask are to answer those Three Ds:

- Where are they located?

- How was the ring lost?

- Where was the ring lost, and how sure are they of its location?

- How big is the search area the ring was lost in?

- Is the area easily accessible?

- Are there any safety issues to be concerned about?

Amongst those questions, you're going to hear answers that will give you enough key points of information to assess whether this has the chance of being a successful ring find or if you should pass. At the end of the day, your time is valuable, and you want to make sure you spend your time on quality jobs. People who call and know for a fact that the ring came off, and in what area it came off, are those "no doubters" you want to go to.

Be wary of jobs where: the caller sounds too interested in your actual process of finding the ring and not at all about finding the ring (they are likely a competitor trying to glean information from you); or the ones that seem hesitant to respond to your questions and are vague about where they lost it (they might not be telling the truth about where the ring was lost); and finally, those that seem to lack emotion and/or don't really appear that upset (it's likely just a prank call).

Not to say that people aren't interested in your process or that they couldn't just be "off" because of the situation. Just make sure you don't fall prey to something that isn't worth your time, and don't get stuck going to a job where the ring was lost in a one-mile square area of the woods, or was thrown out of a car doing one hundred miles an hour down the highway, or was…well, you get the gist. Unless you feel good about it, the chance of finding that ring is so remote that it's almost not worth your time.

PROTIP

Once you and the client agree to the terms of the ring find, ask the client to send you a pinpoint location of the lost ring from Google Maps. This is an excellent way to identify the drop zone and start mapping out your search area.

THE RING QUESTION

Here it is, the question you've been waiting to finally ask. By this time, your client is comfortable with you, and you're getting to the point where you need to negotiate your gratuity. Before that last step can be done, this final bit of information is necessary. Ask them, "Could you tell me a little bit about the ring itself, so I can bring the right equipment."

At this moment, they are forced to either lie and risk the chance of you bringing the wrong equipment and not finding the ring, or telling you the truth and finding the ring. This is where you will find out that it's a platinum ring, with a diamond set around the rim, and a 1.5k diamond on top. This question is the best way to take the information you learned from your earlier questions and set a gratuity rate that matches the scope of your efforts and the worth of this job.

NEGOTIATING THE DEAL

Now, the phone call from your potential client sounds legitimate, you're convinced the person has lost their ring in an identifiable and reasonably-sized area, and you believe that there's a good chance you can find it. Perfect! At this point, all you need to do is negotiate the gratuity.

For some people, this can be very difficult and awkward, but it doesn't have to be. For the first while, I found it extremely uncomfortable accepting a reward. It was only after I realized that I am providing a beneficial and professional service that I began to get comfortable accepting compensation in exchange for my efforts. The three sections below are the best methods to ensure you receive a fair reward for your work, and even how you can turn a $50 find into a $500 one.

One Price, Rain or Shine

Most detectorists prefer this type of arrangement as it's a no-risk fee for the ring finder. You give the client your gratuity rate that they must pay you for the visit—whether you find the ring or not. Calculate your cost for travel time and gas, and select a rate that compensates you for your expenses and rewards you for the work of finding their ring. The average gratuity for this service ranges between $150 and $200.

No Find, No Fee

Believe it or not, I have found this to be the most successful and lucrative style of gratuity. It's risky, but if you play your cards right, ask the right questions, and pick the right customers, you will do very well. The theory behind this one is that people aren't open to paying you much ahead of time, because they're unsure of your ability to actually find their ring.

By telling the client that you won't charge them if you don't find their ring, it eliminates their risk of paying for something that doesn't get found. When you take it one step further and add in, "If I do find the ring, the expected gratuity is $500," it forces the client to ask themselves the question you wanted to all along, "What's the ring really worth—to me?" This is where people (usually) realize that their diamond engagement ring would cost much more than $500 to replace, and are comfortable taking the risk. Negotiating a $50 reward to $500 one, is simply a matter of shifting their perspective.

This iPhone was dropped off a kayak in the middle of a lake. I found it by swimming overhead, following "the Dorothy" spiral search pattern (and using an empty bottle that was tied to a dive weight to mark the drop zone).

7

Earn, not Burn

For a ring finder, there is no greater sense of accomplishment than when it comes to returning someone's lost ring. Most of the time it is a wonderful experience; but, for those few occasions, things can go wrong if you're not prepared. There are individuals out there that do not play by the same rules and will not honor the arrangements you *both* agreed to during the negotiation stage. When I first started ring finding, I was pretty naïve and learned a few things about these people the hard way. This chapter focuses on two ways that you can secure payment for your efforts, without getting burned.

PAY BEFORE YOU PLAY

The best way to guarantee you receive payment for a ring find is to get paid either in full or for a portion of your fee (a deposit), upfront or upon arrival to the location. As the client hasn't yet met you, does not know your skill level, and might even be a little hesitant about this being a scam, you might have better success asking for a deposit.

The amount you can charge for a deposit depends on what your total rate is, but usually falls on the lower-side; between $50 to $100. This method is a nice back-up for you for those rare occurrences when the client does default on the payment. At least you have a portion of your expenses covered. Keep in mind, this slightly contradicts the essence behind the "no find, no fee" method, so you need to either add a disclaimer that the deposit will be returned if the ring is not found, or avoid this and use the swap method below.

THE SWAP

Twice I've been caught where I found a person's lost ring and in a moment of excitement for my find, I handed them their ring only to have them claim they did not actually have the money on hand but would "e-Transfer it later." As you can guess, I never heard from them again, and the money never came.

For this method, once you find the ring, hold onto it until you receive payment for it. Even while taking a picture or a video of the return, stay focused on the ring, and if at all possible, keep the ring in your hand. If for some reason you do hand it to the owner (as they may want to see it up close and verify that it is their ring), ask to see the ring one more time. A good trick for this, is to say you want to take one more close-up photo of the ring, to document your find or share on social media. The ring owner is usually so excited the ring was found that they will hand it back.

At this point, assuming you haven't already received it, you need to ask the owner for the gratuity. It may seem a little awkward at first, but it's the best way to be able to bring your client back down to earth and remind them of their commitment. If they tell you they don't have the money or will e-Transfer it to you later on, kindly respond by saying, "Not a problem. Once I receive that, I will give your ring back as per our agreement." Once you say this, the cash seems to come out of nowhere, or they are able to pay you immediately through e-Transfer.

PROTIP

PayPal, e-Transfers, and a point of sale app and reader on your phone are three ways you can easily accept gratuity payments at a find.

All smiles after I found his fiancée's lost engagement
ring in the snow bank.

8
Your First Find

Your reputation as a ring finder depends not only on your success in finding the ring, but just as importantly on the level of professionalism with which you carry yourself. For every ring finding job, you need to make sure you look the part, show up on time, have the right tools, and do your best to represent your service and the hobby in a positive light. As an ambassador to this hobby, you are expected to always abide by the ring finder code of ethics (these can be found at the end of this book). When you show up for a job, being prepared and acting respectful will not only leave a good impression of ring finders everywhere, but it will make sure you set yourself up for a successful find.

ARRIVAL DO'S AND DON'TS

Arriving to a ring find site and meeting the client for the first time can be a bit intimidating, but by now, you should have the skills and confidence in your abilities to navigate the find with ease. Before you begin the actual find, there are only a few more things you need to do.

Prior to arriving, mind the appearance of yourself, your mode of transportation, and your equipment. Your appearance is the first thing that will further affirm the impression you made on the phone, or cause it to come crumbling down. Wear the proper attire, have a clean vehicle, and make sure your equipment is in working order.

Upon arrival, you need to first go to the door to make your introductions and hand them a business card, and *then* excuse yourself to get your equipment ready. You don't want to be fumbling around with your equipment as you walk up to their door. Be courteous and make small talk, but try and get to work as soon as possible.

When ready, start by asking them to reiterate the story to ensure you are both on the same page. Have them show you, step-by-step, exactly what happened and where it occurred (the drop zone). If possible, have them act it out. Getting the actual visual gives you a better understanding of what happened than what was initially shared during your phone call.

SAFETY FIRST

Before establishing your search area, you need to first do a site survey and safety check. There are so many things that you need to be careful of, so make sure you wear the proper safety attire (as discussed in Chapter 2), and take a walk around.

Look for any overhead or tripping hazards that may be unsafe. Check the area for poison ivy or other infectious plants, and check the ground for any type of debris, sharp objects, garbage, or animal waste. If it's bad enough that you cannot adequately perform the service, don't feel guilty about asking the owner to clean the site before you start.

For everything they clean and remove, have them put it into a paper or plastic bag, for you to run your detector over. You'd be surprised at how many rings are found in a yard waste bag.

REMOVE UNNECESSARY INTERFERENCE

Everything from lawnmowers, boats, bikes, and barbecues can cause interference for your detector, so if there's metal in the area the ring was lost, and the owner is able to move it, request it to be done before you arrive. This saves you time during the find. If the drop zone is located close to a driveway, ask that all vehicles are removed. Good advice is to do a quick visual of the path each vehicle needs to take to get out the driveway. You don't want them to back over their own ring on the way out.

Interference from low-hanging electrical, cable, or telephone lines and underground pipes and buried wires can be a big problem. They can drastically affect the performance of your detector and may make it act erratically or cause false signals; rendering it useless. Adjusting the sensitivity and discrimination settings on the detector will possibly help. To eliminate the chatter from ground interference, use the daisy cutter method (introduced in Chapter 3) and raise the search coil six to eight inches off the ground.

ESTABLISH YOUR SEARCH AREA

Once you've identified the drop zone and have cleared the area from any debris or unnecessary interference, you can use what you learned in Chapter 3 to map out your search area, determine which search method (mowing the lawn, the Dorothy, or the hound dog) you want to use, and begin your search.

This men's vintage black onyx gold ring, with initials, was found on my last swing while searching in an old spring-fed swimming hole.

A beautiful vintage ring that I found while water hunting in front of an old amusement park in the United States.

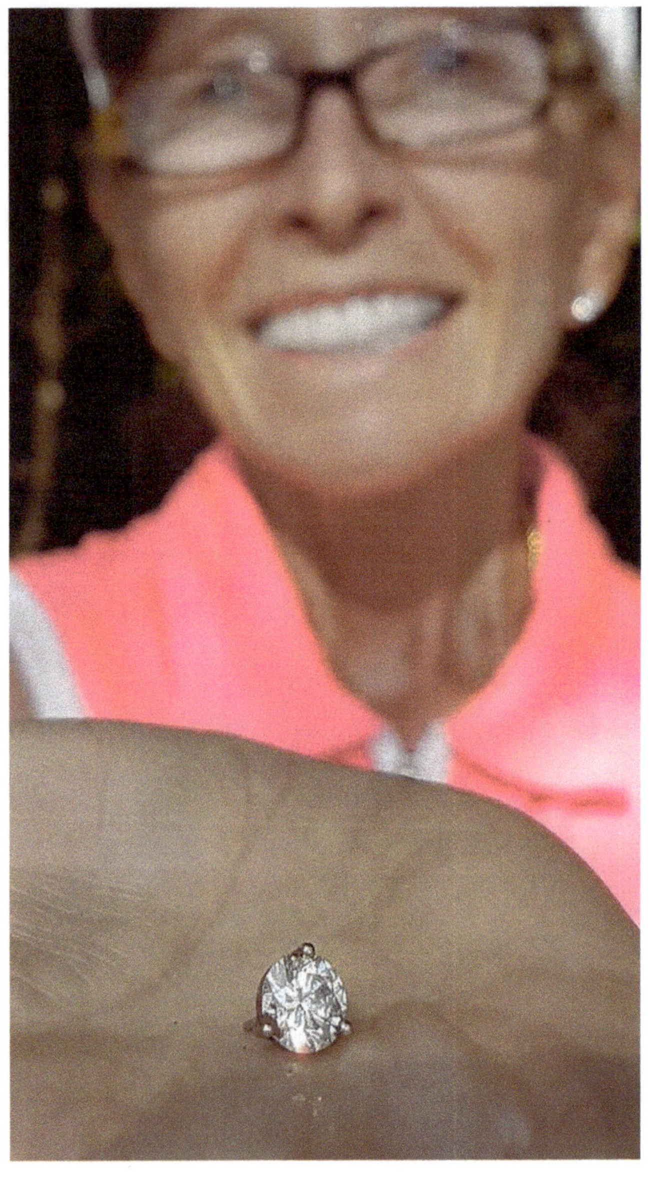

A diamond in the rough. This VVS-grade diamond earring was thought to be "lost forever" in a wooded area, between the greens of a golf course.

9

Capturing the Moment

As discussed in Chapter 5, good quality photos or videos are the absolute best ways to promote your business and build your online presence. Capturing the moment is more than just aiming your camera; it's about sharing a story and creating an emotion through your lens. You need to demonstrate as much about who you are, how you conduct your service, and how you provide value to your clients, through that one moment.

LIVE VIDEO RETURNS

The moment you find a ring and return it is a highly emotional one for your client and is a ring finder's "perfect shot." Sometimes, it can be pretty intense, as the pain of losing their ring was so great that they are filled with overwhelming joy when it's returned. You'll have people hugging you, kissing you, crying, or dancing like they had won the lottery. It is an incredible moment, filled with beautiful visuals, and you don't want to miss it with your camera.

One of the things I have become known for online is the way I record these live ring returns. To replicate the process, there are a few things you need to do. Arrive to a ring find with your fully-charged camera or cell phone in your pocket. You never know when the ring will be found, so be ready. The client is usually preoccupied with looking around for the ring themselves, so nine out of ten times, they won't actually see you find the ring. This is your chance to gently lay your gloves or detector over the ring to hide it. Just note that you should never hide the ring in your pocket—you don't want your integrity coming into question by having someone see this and accuse you of trying to steal it.

Now that you have found the ring and it's safely hidden under your detector or gloves, it's time for the magic! Tell your client that you want to do a short little video interview about their ring and how they lost it. Tell them that it's a great piece to share on social media and that you meant to do it earlier. Have them come over to where you've hidden the ring and start recording.

Begin the video by asking them questions of what the ring looks like, what connections they have to the ring (is it their wedding ring, heirloom, or an old class ring), and how they lost it. You want to paint a picture of their story to help draw the viewer in emotionally. After they've finished with their explanation, ask them what the greatest thing to happen today would be (essentially, what do they want out of this process). They will always reply with "to find the ring." That's the moment you bend down, retrieve the once-lost ring, hold it up in front of the camera, and capture the moment!

TAKING A PHOTO

Great photography is key to being followed on social media and building your audience. Humans are attracted to things that are visual and dramatic, so use your photos to present something that people will love to look at and can easily relate to.

Take a picture of every single ring find; whether it's to keep for your own records, to share on social media, or perhaps, to even put it in a book one day. You never know when you can use it. Try to also take pictures of yourself during the ring find. This helps promote you and show how the ring find is done. Using a chest camera is another way to capture the process while it is happening.

Before you post the photo, make sure its quality is as high as possible. Spend some time editing the photo—make sharpness adjustments, correct the color, change the filter, or even crop it. Most new phones have amazing editing features to help make your photo stand out. If it's in your budget, hire a professional photographer to join you on a couple of hunts.

If you prefer to take your own photos, look for ways that you can enhance the photo before taking it. Play around with your lighting and camera angles, or use natural props such as wood, grass, leaves, rocks, or sand to add depth to a photo and help highlight the ring. Taking a micro shot of a ring on a natural prop with the sun reflecting off the diamond at the perfect angle, helps feature its fine engraved detail and can make any ring (new or old), that was just dug up, look beautiful. If you can and even if it's blurred into the background, try to include your metal detector in your shot. You want viewers to know that this is a metal detecting picture, without trusting them to read the caption.

Finally, never forget to take a photo of the client and the ring you found for them. This is the number one picture people love to see, so don't miss it. This shot, more than anything, connects viewers to the emotion of the story.

SHARING ONLINE

Before you post or share anything, make sure you first obtain your client's permission to use the pictures or videos you took for your advertising purposes. Especially if they are in the shot. Though verbal agreements can be considered legally binding, it's best to get written permission. Have a photo release form printed (you can find examples of these online) and ready for them to sign at the site, or at the very least, get them to send you an email or text to indicate their permission.

To share your photos or videos, remember that you want to use ones that are high-quality and will stand out visually. With your post, add a short, descriptive caption to help explain or give further detail about the ring: where it was found, what kind of ring it was, or perhaps something unique about the client or search.

Depending on what social platform you use, add a few hashtags that are relevant to the picture or video and will help increase its likelihood of getting found. You want to keep the actual hashtags short and easy to read. And select ones that are more commonly used. For inspiration on hashtags you can use, start following other metal detectorists and ring finders online, and watch to see which ones they are using.

A professional ring finder and seasoned diver, my good friend, Ryan Fazekas, displays one of the many beautiful rings he's recovered through the years.

I found this gold 1959 class ring while searching for another lost ring.

I am using the water hunting technique, for shallow waters, while searching for rings in a small lake in Germany.

A beach detector and long-handled scoop are ready for a new day of ring finding.

10

Water Hunting and Dive Detecting

L ess than 10% of all metal detectorists go into the water, and less than 2% of those, dive detect for rings. For someone willing enough to purchase the right equipment and receive the proper training and/or certifications, metal detecting in water is a lucrative way to expand your ring finding service. There are two ways you can hunt for rings in the water: water hunting and dive detecting. The difference between the two is a matter of water depth and equipment.

Water hunting is metal detecting in neck-deep or less water—the swimming area for most people. Rivers, beaches, lakes, and resorts are where majority of your ring finds will occur. Water hunters around the world will be seen hunting in these locations for business (finding rings for those that have lost them) or for pleasure (finding items that have long since lost their owners). You can easily find hundreds of rings or pieces of jewelry that have slipped off people when they were swimming, and if you are unable to return the item to its owner, it can be very profitable for you. A fellow ring finder, based in the

Caribbean, has found just over 7,000 gold rings in his sixteen years in the hobby. Estimating those rings at a very low average of $200 per ring, the total value of his finds is $1.4 million. Yes, you want to get into that water!

Dive detecting is something I coined a few years ago to define metal detecting in water, with the assistance of a scuba diving or hookah breathing apparatus. Of all the scuba divers and metal detectorists in the world, the amount of people in this category falls to less than 1% of that population. As dive detecting requires a scuba certification and more specialized equipment, the rewards for this type of detecting service are much higher than ring finding on land or in shallow waters. For those that offer this service, there is a huge opportunity to build a very successful career for yourself.

EQUIPMENT

Whether you are water hunting or dive detecting for rings, the equipment you need is more specialized than what is required for ring finding on land. Below are the most common items you need to have, before you get below the surface.

Water Detector

There are metal detectors that are capable of detecting on land and in the water; however, most hybrid detectors cannot be submersed more than ten feet deep. Doing so risks leaking issues or causing the machine to flood out. In order to dive detect or water hunt properly, you must have a water detector that is submersible to at least fifteen feet. There are some detectors on the market that are designed to be completely waterproof and fully submersible up to two hundred feet, so it's a matter of choosing one that fits your usage and budget.

Depending where you are detecting, find a metal detector that is designed to perform in both salt and fresh water. Salt water has a high mineral count, and only a few detectors will be able to function properly in it.

Taking care of your metal detector will do wonders for its longevity. After each submersion, rinse it in fresh, soapy water, and then thoroughly dry it off before opening it up to look for water or corrosion around the battery housing. Check that sand has not gotten into any of the interior components or under the search coil cover. If it has, use a toothbrush to clean it out. Lastly, add a little silicone grease to the gaskets, battery seal, and O-ring to keep everything sealed and conditioned.

Dive Shaft

An aftermarket dive shaft is a shorter, more ergonomically-designed shaft that is made to fit on a metal detector. You can swap it out with your regular detector shaft to drastically decrease arm and shoulder fatigue.

Silicone Grease Lubricant

This is one of the most essential things for your water hunting repair kit. A silicone grease lubricant conditions the rubber, plastic, and metal parts of your detecting equipment. Use a cotton swab to apply it to all parts that are subject to drying out, cracking, and corroding.

Scoops

Scoops are a very popular water hunting tool when ring finding on the beach or in shallow water. They are an excellent way to sift out sand when searching for a lost ring. Scoops come in many styles, but the best are made from a strong 304-grade stainless steel which is best for combatting corrosion. Scoops that have a long, carbon fiber handle are lighter to control and prevent the detectorist from having to bend over to retrieve their targets.

Breathing Apparatus

There are three main underwater breathing apparatus options that divers use. The first is a "scuba tank" option, where the diver carries a self-contained air supply. This is the most common and, in my opinion, is the safest option for dive detecting. The self-contained underwater breathing apparatus allows the detectorist the freedom to roam where they want with an untethered and reliable air supply. Divers can use one or two tanks, depending on how much bottom time is required for the recovery.

The next is a "rebreather diving" apparatus; a tankless unit the diver wears. It has a mechanism designed to clean the exhaled air and recycle it back into fresh, breathable air for the diver to use. This form of diving has higher risks but allows for much deeper dives, at extended times.

Finally, a "hookah," or "surface supply," diving system supplies air to the diver through a hose that runs from an air source on the surface, to the regulator that's tethered to them; making it ideal for longer dives. As you are limited to the length of hose, it is meant for shallower waters. The hookah does not

Beach Recovery: Using a Scoop

require scuba diving certifications to use (though it is highly suggested), so it is great for those new to shallow-water diving. The gas-powered options are quite loud, so refrain from using them around resorts or at public beaches.

The ultimate choice between which of these options you should use depends on the environment and situation you are diving in.

Mask and Snorkel

The mask and snorkel combination is a way for water hunters to breath and navigate underwater. Just make sure that your mask seal, lens, and strap are in good condition and that nothing is leaking. Not only can the water irritate your eyes and nose, but it can blur your vision, making it hard to stay aware of your surroundings.

Use a mask defogging gel to prevent your mask lens from fogging up. Prior to use, apply a few drops into your mask, rub it around with your fingers, and briefly rinse under fresh water; ensuring you leave a thin layer of the defogging gel inside the mask. The snorkel should have a comfortable mouth piece, a purge valve to expel the water, and a flexible bottom that allows it to swing out of the detectorist's way when needed.

PROTIP

If you hold your detector in your right hand, place the snorkel on the left-side of your head (or on the right side, if you hold your detector with your left hand). This will prevent your headphone cables from getting caught in your detector.

Diver Down Flag and Dive Float/Ball

Both are used on the water to indicate that there is a diver below and that other vessels should steer clear of the space and proceed with caution.

Diving Suits

A diving suit will help divers stay warm in the water. Made of neoprene, which is a naturally buoyant material, they are designed to be light, flexible, and protect the diver. When choosing a diving suit, make sure you find one that is the proper size for your body and is made for the type of diving you're doing. There are two main types of diving suits: dry and wet.

Drysuits are used in colder waters and will keep you completely dry. They are designed to be bigger, to accommodate a fleece base layer, and to assist in its main function of keeping a diver warm under the water.

Wetsuits are available in long or short options and are used to keep the internal core temperate of the water hunter or diver comfortable. The most preferred for this hobby, are the shorty wetsuits. They won't over-heat you and are easier to put on than full wetsuits, as they don't provide full coverage. However, if the water is filled with things that could bite, cut, or sting you, it might be a good idea to wear a full suit.

To store your diving suit, hang it inside a dry, warm environment—not in your garage. This will help it to properly dry out, stay free of mold, and prevent critters from chewing up the material. Cleaning it with warm water and a wetsuit or drysuit cleanser (or baby shampoo), on a regular basis will help keep it fresh.

Buoyancy Compensator

Also known as a buoyancy control device, or "BC", the buoyancy compensator is a vest with an inflatable bladder that divers wear underwater. It will help you establish neutral buoyancy underwater and positive buoyancy when it's time to surface. This piece of diving equipment is manually controlled, so it requires an extreme amount of skill and attention during operation. Practice your skills at your community pool or with your local dive club, and don't go into open water until you know how to properly use it.

Gloves

Some water hunters prefer not to wear gloves, as it takes away feeling in their fingers and can inhibit their sense of touch for the ring. However, using a pair of thin, nitrile-coated gloves, that you can get at any home improvement store, will allow you to still feel the ring and keep you protected from slicing your hand or fingers on sharp objects. For even better protection of your hands, or for those early spring or cold-water dives, you can opt for a pair of thicker, waterproof neoprene gloves.

Footwear

Always wear something on your feet when ring finding in the water. A low-cut neoprene paddling booty, that fits snug on your foot and has a good outsole, is an excellent choice. They give you grip on wet surfaces and will protect your feet from injury. Check these annually for any tears or holes, and throw away any pair that have. You'd hate to have to end your dive short because a piece of glass or coral cut you through a hole.

Finds Pouch

Unlike with ring finding on land, when searching for rings underwater you want to make sure you have a finds pouch to put any rings or jewelry you found inside. It belts around your waist and is just large enough to place coins and rings inside the zippered compartment. Your hands will be full of equipment, and you don't want to drop the ring you just found. A finds bag will keep them safe as you swim back up to the surface. Alternatively, many divers will bring a small carabiner with them. Clipped to either your BC (at chest level) or to the inside of your finds pouch, it is another way to secure any rings you've found.

TAKING THE CALL

The process of accepting and pricing a ring finding job in the water is much the same as explained in Chapter 6. You need to ask the Three Ds (distance, difficulty, and do they know where it is), but you also need consider the conditions of the water. In poor weather or with high waves, ring finding is almost impossible and extremely dangerous. It is better for you to wait a day or two for the water to calm down before searching for the ring. When a ring falls off someone's finger and lands on the soil or sand below, it won't get moved around by the water, it will just embed itself deeper into the sand. The task of finding the ring can wait for safer conditions.

TECHNIQUES

When it comes to searching for rings under water, the search patterns are basically the same as the ones you use on land, that were discussed in Chapter 3. However, it's the obstacles that are much different. Rather than branches, leaves, and debris to worry about, you now have people, jet skis, and boats to contend with. Be safe in the water and always remain aware of your surroundings.

There are two main techniques a dive detectorist uses to displace sand and recover their target: "**fanning**" and "**patting**." When fanning, divers literally fan their hand back-and-forth over the target to make a large hole. This method is great for targets that are buried deep below the sand level. For a shallow target, the patting method is more effective. With this technique, divers pat their hand over top of the target. This allows them to quickly make a small hole with less effort.

With either technique, the ring will eventually pop out of the hole or will move closer to the top. Once the sand has settled, you will be able to see it or easily feel for it with your fingers. Both techniques move a large amount of sand very quickly and are the most effective ways to find a ring. It is highly recommended that you wear gloves when using these techniques. There's always the chance that a nail or piece of glass might be in the way and can easily slice your hand.

SAFETY IN THE WATER

Be careful when ring finding in the water, and remember that the most dangerous thing in the water is man. Power boats, fishing boats, jet skis, paddle boards, party boats, and surfers will take you out long before a shark ever will. A good strategy is to follow the **one-on-one-off rule**, which basically means keeping one headphone on one ear and one headphone off the other ear. This will allow you to more effectively hear for oncoming watercrafts.

Dive Detecting

Using a dive float or a diver down ball or flag to mark that you are diving underneath is a good idea, but can sometimes also create a danger. I can't tell you the number of times jet skiers have come over the top of my head to check out my diver down ball, because they thought it was a lost beach ball. Just be careful and use your own common sense.

Always dive with a certified partner, and communicate a dive plan before you go into the water. Know where you will be detecting, how long you plan to go for, and where you will meet if you lose each other. Make sure that someone on the surface is also aware of your plan.

Work out a set of signals that allows you to easily communicate with each other underwater. My dive partner and I use squealers (underwater whistles that connect to your airline hose) and have created our own set of signals. Three quick blasts for, "Where are you?" Two quick blasts mean, "I found a ring!" Three long blasts indicate, "Danger overhead!"

DISCLAIMER

Dive detecting is a dangerous sport. Before you go into the open water, make sure you've received the proper certifications and training, know how to use your equipment (and check that it is working properly before every dive), and are aware of international diving rules and regulations for the location you're detecting in.

Recovering a lost ring while enjoying a beautiful Canadian sunset.

11

Ring Finding Through the Seasons

As you've gathered by now, ring finding is a year-round hobby. Each season has its own nuances, specific to the conditions, so it's worth it to be prepared for each season in which you are hunting.

SPRING

It's common for people's fingers to shrink in cold, wet weather, so the rainy months of spring are a typical time to receive calls for lost rings. These conditions also mean that ring finding in the spring can be a bit of a wet and muddy job. Always have a pair of hiking boots with excellent traction, gel filled knee pads, nitrile-dipped gloves, a warm hat, and a spare raincoat at this time of year.

Spring is also a great time to do an annual assessment of your equipment and make any necessary changes or repairs. Replace items that are unfixable, and tune up items that aren't working properly.

SUMMER

As it's beach season, you won't receive a lot of land calls during the summer months. Most of the calls made are about rings lost in the water or at the beach. This is great for water detectorists, because there's no place better to look for rings and make some money on a hot, summer day than at the beach.

After each visit to the beach, wash down all of your equipment with some fresh water. As discussed in Chapter 10, sand gets into everything, and it's critical you remove it before it causes damage to your metal detector and equipment.

FALL

Fall is a very interesting time of year because you can get any number of calls about rings being lost on land, at the beach, or in the water. This, for obvious reasons, is the number one time of year you want to bring a rake in your vehicle.

WINTER

The colder climates of winter cause fingers to shrink, and many a ring will come flying off when someone removes their gloves. This makes winter the number one season for rings being lost on land and the busiest season for a ring finder. You might even want to adjust the frequency of your online advertising at this time of year to account for the increased amount of calls. Another reason that winter is such a great season for ring finders is that people tend to "migrate" to warm tropical beaches. For a ring finder willing to travel, it's a perfect opportunity to stay warm and find rings.

This 30-inch 18k gold Crucifix necklace was found in two inches of water, on my last swing of a long day of ring finding.

This gentleman had almost given up hope of finding his platinum wedding ring. Using the "daisy cutter" swing style, I was easily able to find his ring.

The Ring Finder Code of Ethics

Properly filling your holes and obeying the local laws and trespassing signs should be followed by all metal detectorists. The following list is the ring finder code of ethics that should be followed by all professionals, on land and in water.

- I will be an ambassador to our hobby, and I will treat each client and colleague with courtesy and respect.

- I will conduct myself with honesty.

- I will respect the property on which I am detecting.

- I will refrain from detecting on any historical or archaeological sites without permission.

- I will not damage any property and will ensure I leave it better than the way I found it; if possible, removing garbage or dangerous objects that might cause harm to others.

- I will not keep any rings that do not belong to me, and I will make every effort possible to return them to their rightful owners.

- I will at all times be aware of my own safety and the safety of others.

- I will mentor and give good advice, to the best of my ability, to uplift and honor the hobby of ring finding.

Dive Detecting in the Caribbean.

A Final Word from the Author

Ring finding is a game of patience, and knowing how much faith a person has put in you to find their ring can be a lot of pressure. As you well know, there are times when you will not be able to find the ring you're looking for, and the disappointment you will feel may weigh heavily upon you. Alternatively, the owner might find their own ring before you do, which is great, but means you are out of a gratuity. You must prepare yourself for the possibility of either of these happening, because eventually—it will. Just be thankful it wasn't while being broadcast on a national radio station (yes, this happened to me before).

Albert Einstein said, "Strive not to be a success, but rather to be of value." As a ring finder, you have acquired an ability to be of great value to others, and by using a metal detector honestly and wisely, you will unite people with their long-lost rings. There's something to be said about someone who can provide such joy through their work. As you embark on your journey of becoming a ring finder, I encourage you to keep learning and go on as many finds as possible to hone your skills. Don't let the "no finds" discourage you, open yourself up to the opportunities of this new community you've joined, and uphold the ring finder code of ethics.

In the sincerest expression of gratitude, I want to thank you for purchasing and reading my book. It is my pleasure to now congratulate and welcome you as a colleague and fellow ring finder. Good luck my friends!

Using a water detector, this beautiful gold ring was found fresh from the surf after hearing that perfect "sound of gold."

This exquisite, early 1900s jade ring is an example of how long a ring can be lost, before being found. In this case, just over 100 years.

Glossary

Arm Cuff. The u-shaped component on a metal detector. Using a strap to keep it secured around your arm, it helps to reduce neck and arm strain and keeps the detector steady as you sweep it back and forth.

Buoyancy Compensator (BC). A vest with an inflatable bladder that divers wear underwater. It will help you establish neutral buoyancy underwater and positive buoyancy when it's time to surface.

Coil Head. See "Search Coil."

Control Box. The "brains" of a metal detector. It houses the battery, microprocessor, controls, circuitry, and speaker. Its function is to run the detector and process all audio and visual information for the user.

Daisy Cutter. An "elevated" swing technique used to reduce ground interference to locate surface finds. Performed by swinging the detector coil six to eight inches above ground.

Detection Depth. The maximum depth at which a metal detector can locate a metal target in the ground. The size of the search coil and ground composition are variables that will affect this.

Detector Cable. This electronic cable connects the search coil to the control box. It relays the information from the coil head to the control box, which is then processed to the detector display screen. Proper installation will prevent the rotation of the coil head from pinching and eventually damaging the cable.

Detector Programs/Modes. Most metal detectors come equipped with factory-installed programs such as: All Metals, Beach, Coin Finding, and Ring Finding. These programs assist the detectorist with retrieving their target. Simply press the mode you want and being.

Detector Settings. Common metal detector settings are on/off, detection depth, sensitivity, volume, discrimination, threshold, and pinpoint mode. Refer to the detector's manual or ask your dealer to properly set up your detector prior to use.

Detectorist. A person that uses a metal detector.

Discrimination. A metal detector setting that can be adjusted to accept or ignore certain metals. Low discrimination can be noisy, but will allow for deeper targets to be located. High discrimination will allow for a fast recovery of a surface find or recently lost ring.

Display or Screen. Provides visual information about your targets. Numbers shown will help you correctly identify targets in or on the ground.

Dive Detecting. Underwater metal detecting with a submersible metal detector and air supply.

Dive Float/Ball or Diver Down Flag. Markers used by dive detectorists to indicate that there is a diver below and that other vessels should steer clear of the space and proceed with caution.

Diver Down Flag. See "Dive Float/Ball."

Drop Zone. The location a ring was presumably dropped.

Fanning. A water recovery technique where a diver literally fans their hand back-and-forth over the target to make a large hole. This method is great for targets that are buried deep below the sand level.

Ferrous Metal Targets: Ferrous targets contain iron and are usually not a desirable target. Items such as nails, spikes, and scrap metal fall under this category.

Finds Pouch. Attached to its own belt and worn around the waist, a finds pouch easily carries your targets when detecting. A waterproof version exists for water hunters and dive detectorists.

Golden Circle: Used in "The Dorothy" technique, this is the circular area you mark out around where the ring was presumed to be lost (the "drop zone"). Usually fifteen feet in diameter; approximately the size of an above ground pool.

Gratuity. The amount of money (or tip) that a client provides to you in exchange for your ring finding service.

Gratuity-based Service. A Service that has no base price and is funded solely by the gratuity given by the client to the provider of the service.

Gridding. See "Search Patterns."

(Ground) Chatter. Sporadic signals a metal detector makes; caused by electromagnetic interference from highly mineralized or "trashy" ground. Anything from lawnmowers, boats, bikes, metal, and trash can cause interference for your detector.

Hookah or Surface Supply. An underwater breathing apparatus option for dive detectorists. It supplies air to the diver through a hose that runs from an air source on the surface, to the regulator that's tethered to them. It is ideal for longer dives.

Hybrid Metal Detector. A machine capable of metal detecting on land and in water.

Influencers. People on social media that have established a reputation for their expertise and knowledge on a particular topic.

Interference. When a metal detector acts erratically due to an outside electromagnetic disturbance.

Karat (k) and Carat (ct). Karat (k), is a unit of purity of gold. Carat (ct) is a unit of weight to measure the size a diamond or gemstones.

Land-based Metal Detector. The most common metal detector used. Typically, designed with a very low frequency (VLF) system. Higher-end units are able to recover many targets on land, up to twelve inches in the ground. They are unable to fully submerge in water.

Metal Detector. An electromagnetic device that gives an audible or visual signal when it's close to metal. Used to find buried metal objects. Comes in various land-based, hybrid, and water-based options.

Mowing the Lawn. The simplest and most commonly-used metal detecting search pattern. When done correctly, this pattern resembles a person "mowing the lawn" to recover a lost item.

No Find, No Fee. At times, a very lucrative gratuity-based strategy used by ring finders. This strategy offers the service for free if the ring is not found; yet, may result in a higher yield if the ring is found.

Non-ferrous Metal Targets. Most precious metals such as gold, silver, and platinum are non-ferrous. These metals do not contain iron.

One-On-One-Off Rule. A water safety strategy which means keeping one headphone on one ear and one headphone off the other ear. This will allow you to more effectively hear for oncoming danger.

Patting. A water recovery technique where a diver pats their hand over top of the target. This allows them to quickly make a small hole, with less effort.

Pay Before You Play. The safest way for a ring finder to receive a gratuity. This technique requires the detectorist to receive payment either in full or for a portion of their fee (deposit), upfront or upon arrival to the location.

Pinpointer Probe. A small, handheld metal detector that's the size of a thin flashlight. It either vibrates or emits a tone when it comes in close proximity to a metal target.

Rebreather Diving. A tankless underwater breathing apparatus option for dive detectors. It has a mechanism designed to clean the exhaled air and recycle it back into fresh, breathable air for the diver to use. This form of diving has higher risks, but allows for much deeper dives, at extended times.

Screen. See "Display."

Scuba Tank. The most common underwater breathing apparatus option where the diver carries a self-contained air supply. This allows the detectorist the freedom to roam where they want with an untethered and reliable air supply.

Search Area. An area the detectorist will use a metal detector in, to look for a lost ring.

Search Coil or Coil Head. The flat, circular disk located at the end of your metal detector shaft. The wires inside the search coil create an electromagnetic field that reacts with metal objects in the ground. That information is then sent to the control box where it is processed into audio and visual information for the user.

Search Patterns or Gridding. Organized and systematic ring finding techniques. Common techniques are mowing the lawn, the Dorothy, the hound dog, fanning, and patting.

Shaft. The center pole of the metal detector that all other components connect to. The shaft comes in two adjustable parts, the upper and lower sections, that allow the user to match it to their height as well as the intended use of the machine. Shorter shafts are best for diving and detecting in water; whereas, a longer shaft is best for detecting on land.

Signal or Tone. The audio sound your detector uses to communicate that it has located a metal target.

Soil Plug. A chunk of soil that's dug out of a hole and is flipped over to reveal your ring or target.

Target. A word used to describe the (metal) objects a metal detectorist is either looking for or has found.

Target ID: The visual identification displayed on the detector screen that will give you more information on, and help identify, your target.

Test Garden. An area a detectorist plots out to bury different metal targets, at varying depths, to practice using their metal detector with different techniques.

The Dorothy. A spiral search pattern (done as a circular sweep of the area) that metal detectorists can use to locate a lost item. This is best used when time is of the essence or you're running low on daylight.

The Hound Dog. A ring finding search pattern, also known as "freestyling," which bases its technique on the detectorist's intuition.

Three Ds. When assessing the worth of a ring find and the amount required for a gratuity, use the Three Ds: distance, difficulty, and do they know where it is.

Tone. See "Signal."

Water Hunting. Metal detecting in (neck-deep or less) water. This is done by either walking or snorkeling in the water.

Water-based Metal Detector. A completely submersible metal detector that is capable of functioning at depths of up to 200 feet deep in the water.

The ricochet ring. Sometimes, you need to search in the opposite place from where your client "knew" they lost it. This ring ricocheted off the roof of a car and was found sixty feet in the opposite direction, from where it was first suspected to have been lost.

This newly-purchased 10th anniversary diamond ring came off during a midnight swim.

Acknowledgments

I couldn't begin to thank all the people who have influenced and supported me in the writing of this book without starting with my dad—Mytro (Pete) Zazulyk. When I was a young boy, he was the first rescue diver for our local fire department. It was his sense of adventure and ability to help so many others that inspired me to be the person I am today.

Secondly, I have the most wonderful wife and daughters anyone could have. Kelly, Natalie, and Olivia, you are my oxygen and why I'm able to look forward to each day with so much happiness. Your support, prayers, and constant reminders to "not do anything stupid" remind me each day of how much you love me. An additional thank you to Natalie—she is a talented photographer and provided some of photos for this book, including the cover photo. In addition, my daughters have amazing guys in their lives who are unwavering in their support of me and my passion for this hobby. Thank you so much, Patrick and Marcos. All of you make me so proud!

It's important for me to also mention my extended family in Germany, the Rößlers and Merwarths. You show me nothing but kindness and encouragement as I set out the door, with detector in hand, each time I visit you in Germany. Danke schöne.

It is said that if you could count the number of close, trusted friends in your life on one hand, you're blessed. I seem to have that blessing in abundance. Those I am lucky enough to call my close friends, have been a big part of my success and for what's on the pages of this book. My dear friend, John Scarfo; you are like a brother to me, and you and your family have shown me constant love and support for the twenty (plus) years I have known you. I love you guys. My detecting and dive partner, Ryan Fazekas; you are second to none with a metal detector. The advancements your company (Anderson Detector Shafts) have made to the metal detecting shaft, shows your dedication to the improvement of this hobby. Thank you for pushing me to be the best detectorist I could possibly be. I truly value the many days we spend in the water, here and in the Caribbean, searching for those elusive rings. You and your wonderful family mean more to me than you know. Thank you!

Ring finding and metal detecting have brought me down some unexpected paths to find a few pretty amazing treasures along the way. I often tell people that the greatest treasures I have found are the friends I've met: Pete Anderson, Jack Summers, Alison Walker, Joe Loiacono, Butch and Anita Holcombe, and my little shadow, Joe Fox. No gold ring could ever match our friendship… well, maybe a really big one. Kidding! You are all a *true* treasure to me.

To my mentor, Richard Eldon. Though our time together was short, the lessons I learned from you are invaluable. It's in your memory that I mentor fellow detectorists, as you did for me.

Chris Turner, your tireless efforts to promote the hobby have helped elevate ring finders everywhere. Your organization, the RingFinders, has been a great support for myself and many others in the industry—helping members return over 5,000 lost rings to their rightful owners. Being a member of the RingFinders is an excellent way for those new to the hobby to advertise themselves and promote their service.

To my talented and ever-patient editor, Lacy Lieffers at One Leaf Editing; this book would not exist without your kindness and amazing skills. I cannot thank you enough for your guidance and endless hours of work in the writing of this book.

Finally, I would like to thank all of the people who have asked me to find their rings. I've literally gone around the world meeting you, and I have formed some of the best friendships I could ever imagine. If not for you, I would not have the wonderful stories, photographs, and experiences displayed throughout this book. Being a part of that incredible moment when you were reunited with your lost ring is something I do not take lightly and will always remember. I want to thank you so much for that opportunity and your trust.

You are *all* the reason I am the Ring Finder. Thank you.